KARATE KICKING

W9-CHP-814

KARATE KICKING

Keith Vitali
Kent Mitchell

Contemporary Books, Inc.
Chicago

Library of Congress Cataloging in Publication Data

Vitali, Keith.
    Karate kicking.

    Includes index.
    1. Karate.   I. Mitchell, Kent.   II. Title.
GV1114.3.V573   1983   796.8'153   83-7683
ISBN 0-8092-5494-8

Photography by Norman DeWalt

Copyright © 1983 by Keith Vitali and Kent Mitchell
All rights reserved
Published by Contemporary Books, Inc.
180 North Michigan Avenue, Chicago, Illinois 60601
Manufactured in the United States of America
Library of Congress Catalog Card Number: 83-7683
International Standard Book Number: 0-8092-5494-8

Published simultaneously in Canada by Beaverbooks, Ltd.
195 Allstate Parkway, Valleywood Business Park
Markham, Ontario L3R 4T8 Canada

Contents

To my parents, Joseph and Dorothy Vitali,
for all their love and support.

Foreword

Keith Vitali and I met in 1972 as young students in South Carolina, even before we made black belt. Both of us were determined to learn, achieve, and succeed in karate, and we spent long hours viewing our idols—Joe Lewis, Bill Wallace, Jeff Smith, and Dan Anderson—on film, talking to our peers at tournaments, trying to acquire new perspectives on style, strategy, and technique. We spent even more hours in actual training.

In 1977 this all paid off. Keith was recognized for his fine teaching abilities and talent in the ring by karate entrepreneur Joe Corley, who hired him to be chief instructor of his Atlanta schools. The move also gave Keith the means to pursue national competition, and he was named the number one fighter in America for three straight years.

Keith's unparalleled excellence in the ring pushed him to the top. Never before had we seen so clean a technician, so spirited a fighter, so intelligent a strategist. He proved to all that the number one fighter in the nation had a polish, a shine that will be difficult to match anytime in the near future.

Keith has yet to be surpassed as the "winningest" grand champion ever. Top honors have gone to him in such memorable tournaments as the PKA Nationals, the Mid-Americas, the Oklahoma City Nationals, and twice in both the Battle of Atlanta and the AKA Grand Nationals, to name only a few. While most top-rated black belts pride themselves on becoming models for young students, Keith adds yet another exclusive group to this list. Not only do newcomers want to imitate him and his style; so do seasoned veterans. Competitors with many more years under their belts have attempted to make effective the now famous, patented Vitali Back Fist and Side Kick.

With all the victories about which he could boast, Keith has never lost his humility. He has an air about him that attracts fans everywhere. His winning smile and personable attitude make him one of the most popular men in karate.

As a fighter, Keith Vitali is one of the best. As a man, Keith Vitali possesses the finest quality of character to be found. And as a friend, there will never be another like him.

Mike Genova

Acknowledgments

I would like to thank James Chason, Rick Mitchell, and my wife, Cindy for their assistance with the photography. A kind thanks to Norman DeWalt for lending his photography skills.

Thanks go to my friend and student, Kent Mitchell, who cowrote this book with me as well as *Karate for Beginners,* also published by Contemporary Books, Inc. Kent has the gift of being able to transfer thoughts and actions to paper in a clear, concise manner that is easy to read and understand.

A special thanks goes to Mike Genova for his foreword and for his friendship over the years. Mike has experienced along with me my lows in karate as well as my highs, because he was always there by my side.

A thank you also is in order for all of the fine kickers in karate who have had direct influence on the way kicks are used in today's sport. Just a few of the great kickers who have had that effect—only the ones that I had a chance to view in action—include Joe Lewis, Bill Wallace, Chuck Norris, Joe Corley, Mike

Genova, Dan Anderson, Ray McCallum, Larry Kelley, John Longstreet, and Vernon Johnson.

A special thanks is also in order to John Roper, my instructor at the University of South Carolina who promoted me to Black Belt, for his emphasis on the basics of the kicking art.

1

Introduction

It's quite possible that you have seen, at one time or another, kicks in the movies, on television, or at tournaments that seem downright impossible. The thought could have gone through your head that the people doing the kicks were abnormal, so much more gifted than you that it was futile even to try to copy them. But what if you found out that there was a way to learn how to kick like the champions? Would you give it a try? Can you picture yourself attacking an opponent taller and faster than you with a Round Kick to the head, followed quickly by a Side Kick and another Round Kick to the head? Can you see yourself doing that?

It's not impossible. In fact, all it takes is a knowledge of some specialized drills plus a lot of hard practice. The secret will come in the following pages, and once you've looked at it, you will probably react this way: "Now, why didn't I think of that?" The simplicity probably helps keep the secret.

The entire premise of this book is that knowledge is power, that you understand your kicking game. Since the legs are longer and stronger and you walk on them all day, they are much more powerful weapons than someone's punches.

We will be working on a series of kicking combinations that have been proven in the ring, in tournaments, and elsewhere. The idea is to start with single kicks and execute the proper form with them, then to progress to double kicks and not only deliver pretty kicks but use them intelligently as well. There is much more to kicking than knowing how. You must know *when* to kick, too, and *why* you are using certain kicks or combinations.

By adopting the knowledge contained in this book and working regularly on the drills, you should see an improvement in a matter of months.

2

Stretching for Flexibility

As you progress to the high, advanced multiple kicks, stretching becomes even more important than before. The extremely quick movements require the utmost in flexibility for speed and to prevent injury. Tight muscles are prone to tear when subjected to the kind of stress that accompanies multiple kicks. You also need a flexible body to be able to deliver two or three techniques to the head while maintaining an upright body position, ready to deliver punches if the opportunity presents itself.

Start with an easy warm-up, a minute of running in place, or a couple of minutes of jumping rope, followed by another minute of jumping jacks. While the legs are resting and you are returning to normal breathing, loosen the neck muscles by rotating the head 10 times in each direction. Follow this with upper body twists: spread the feet to shoulder width, grasp your hands directly in front of your breastbone, arms parallel to the floor, and twist your upper body from left to right. As you turn your body, turn your head and try to see an object directly behind you. A varia-

3

Keith Vitali's wife, Cindy, and the ultimate flexibility.

Spread the feet to shoulder width, then turn the body to right and back to left.

tion is to turn your body while your head continues to face the front. Do 15 repetitions of each.

Next, do about 20 hip twists in each direction. Again, start with your feet about shoulder width apart and begin to move your hips in circles while your head and feet remain constant in relation to each other. It's similar to tacking a piece of string to the floor, putting a tennis ball midway down the string and swinging the ball in circles. The top and bottom remain still.

Now that your body is warmed up, begin stretching the legs. The first exercise will work on the hamstrings and groin muscles. Place the feet slightly farther apart than shoulder width, bend forward from the waist, and try to touch your palms to the floor. Don't strain; stretch gently until you feel a slight pulling of the muscles. Hold this position for 30 seconds. During that time you will notice your hands getting closer to the floor as the muscles in

Bend from the waist down and touch the floor with your hands. Then bend and touch the right knee, then the left knee, with your head.

your legs and back stretch out. Next, bend at the waist and try to touch your nose or forehead to your left knee. Hold for 30 seconds and repeat to the right knee. Be careful to bend only from the waist and not to curl the back or tuck the head in. Both can cause lower back injuries.

Spread your feet to about twice shoulder width and bend forward again. Bend straight down and try to touch your elbows to the floor. Don't force this. Just bend over and let your body hang down. If your elbows touch, that's fine, but don't lean forward or lose your balance and fall forward. Hold for 30 seconds and then repeat the moves to each knee, holding each for 30 seconds.

Spread your feet to twice shoulder width **(A)**, bend at the waist and touch head or elbows to the floor **(B)**, then to the right **(C)** and left **(D)** knees.

A

The next step is to allow your feet to spread out until your muscles stop the movement or your body touches the floor. The latter is called a Chinese or Russian split and is not easily attained. Much daily work is required to loosen muscles that have had all your life to reach their respective stages of tightness. As you slide your feet out to the sides, bend forward at the waist and rest your upper body on the floor. Also, when you feel you've gone about as far as you can go, rotate your legs so that your body is resting on your heels with the toes up. This will allow further stretch. If you can't split all the way to the floor, ease yourself into a sitting position, keeping the legs spread, and lean as far forward as possible. You will progress from barely being able to lean to finally resting your head on the floor. Hold this position for 30 seconds, then lean to the left as far as possible and hold for another 30 seconds. Again, you might not make much progress at first, but as you continue, your body will grow looser, and soon your head will be able to rest on your knee. Repeat to the right knee.

If your muscles are loose enough, you will be able to do the Russian, or Chinese, split **(A)**. Lean forward and touch the floor in front of you **(B)**, then lean to one side and touch your head to your knee **(C)**. Repeat the process to the opposite knee **(D)**.

Draw the right foot in to the groin **(A)**, then lean forward and touch your head to your left knee **(B)**; repeat the process to the right **(C** and **D)**.

Sit up, and slowly draw your feet together, keeping the legs straight. Draw in the left leg and lean forward to touch the right knee with your nose. Hold for 30 seconds, switch legs, and repeat to the left leg. Extend both legs in front of you with feet together, lean forward from the waist (do not bend the back), and try to touch your head to your knees. Don't force this; just relax and lean forward for 30 seconds.

Stand up, shake your legs to loosen the muscles further, and then spread your feet to twice shoulder width again. Turn your body to the right and swivel your feet so that your right foot is facing in the direction you are looking and your left, or rear, foot is touching the floor on a line from the big toe to the heel (the side kick position). Bend your right leg, keep your left leg straight, and try to keep your body upright. Hold for 30 seconds and repeat to the left. This further stretches your groin muscles. Go back to the position facing right and this time allow your rear leg to slide back as far as it can. If your body touches the floor, you are in the American split. Don't force this; take your time and work out to it. Repeat the move in the opposite direction.

By now your body should be ready for some high kicking. If you have never used these stretching methods, you'll probably get some immediate results in kicking higher than ever. By working on these stretches daily, you will find your kicks getting higher more easily, with a great deal more speed and less effort.

After accomplishing the American split **(A)**, one step further is to lean forward and touch your head to your knee **(B)**; repeat to the other leg **(C and D)**.

3

Basic Kicks

Find the best karate kicker in the world, the man who can deliver several techniques in one combination—Roundhouse Kick, Side Kick, Hook Kick, without ever putting the foot down and with focus and power—and you'll discover a man who has mastered the basics.

There is an old cliché that says that a building is no stronger than its foundation. Tired it may be, but true, and certainly in karate. The person with the most sound basic techniques will be the person who also has the best multiple kicks. One follows the other.

A quick review of the basic kicks and some drills to improve them won't be wasted. One of the best ways to improve form and focus in any kick is the slow-motion drill. This should be done once or twice a week in order to build up certain key muscles while etching the moves of the particular technique into your brain. Full-speed drills into the air, at a partner, or at your own image in a mirror will help develop focus and speed. Kicks into heavy bags or bags held by a partner will help build up power. Practice all three.

Forward fighting stance, front view.   Forward fighting stance, side view.

Side fighting stance, side view.   Side fighting stance, front view.

FRONT KICK: Start in the forward stance **(A)**, raise the knee **(B)**, cock the foot, and thrust the weapon to the target **(C)**; return **(D)**.

FRONT KICK

Usually, the Front Kick is the first one a new student learns. Although it seems so easy and comes so early in training, a Front Kick, by itself, can still be a winner at times if it is done to perfection.

The slow-motion drill is done in four parts.

1. From the forward fighting stance, raise the knee to waist level or higher and point the foot downward while curling

the toes back in order to expose the weapon (ball of the foot).

2. Slowly thrust the weapon to the target and hold for five seconds.
3. Return to the cocked, or channeled, position.
4. Return to the forward fighting stance.

Do five repetitions on each leg. Follow this with focused one-count drills, concentrating on speed and form, keeping your hands in the fighting position, and aiming the kick at a specific point on your partner or at your own image in the mirror. Do at least 15 kicks on each leg.

A

B

SIDE KICK, side view: Start in the side stance **(A)**, slide up the rear foot **(B)**, channel the weapon **(C)**, and thrust the weapon to the target **(D)**.

SIDE KICK

There's no way of getting around the fact that it is difficult to follow certain techniques with a Side Kick. When you first try a Side Kick–Round Kick drill or a Swing Kick–Side Kick you will feel tremendously awkward. The only way to correct this is to execute the Side Kick perfectly.

SIDE KICK, front view: Starting in the side stance **(A)**, slide up the rear foot **(B)**, channel the weapon (note heel and buttock position) **(C)**, and thrust the heel to the target (note toes facing down) **(D)**; return **(E)**.

First, do the slow-motion drill, which also helps build up the hip muscle that will be a key to multiple kicks.

1. From the side stance, slide the rear foot to the front foot and at the same time turn the rear foot so that the toes are pointing to your rear.
2. Cock, or channel, your leg so that the knee is high and the weapon (the heel) is pointing at the target. Seen from the target's point of view, the heel is lined up with the buttocks.
3. Slowly extend the weapon to the target and hold for a count of five. Be sure that the leg is locked out and fully extended and that the hip is turned over so that the toes are pointed downward.
4. Return to the channeled position and hold (this is important to train you to recoil after a kick instead of kicking and dropping your weapon).
5. Return to the side stance.

Do five repetitions on each leg. Follow with 15 full-speed kicks, working on speed and focus and concentrating on recoil. Also work at least once a week on power kicks, either at a heavy bag or working with a partner. Occasionally have your partner move around as though you were actually fighting to add to the realism of the drill.

B C

D E

ROUNDHOUSE KICK

The Roundhouse Kick figures prominently in many multiple techniques, as the first, second, or third kick in a combination. Execution must be perfect or you will be so out of position for follow-up kicks that they will be useless.

Now do the slow-motion drill.

1. Start in the side stance and slide the rear foot to the front foot, turning the rear foot so that the toes are facing to the rear.
2. Raise your knee, but this time keep it in line with the target and cock your foot so that the weapon (the instep) is exposed.
3. Move the weapon to the target, holding the knee in position, and turn the hip over slightly at the point of contact (this is for power), holding for a count of five.
4. Return along the same path to the channeled position.
5. Return to the side stance.

Do this five times on each leg. Follow this with 15 sliding front-

ROUNDHOUSE KICK, side view: Start in the side stance **(A)** and slide up (note rear foot position) **(B)**; channel the weapon, with the knee in line with the target **(C)**. Keeping the knee in the same position, in line with the target, move the weapon (instep) to the target **(D)** and return **(E)**.

leg kicks on each leg, emphasizing speed and focus, using the head as a target. The kick should almost look like a flipper, but the hip motion will give it unbelievable power. Also practice the back-leg version of the Roundhouse Kick, which is more of a power kick than a speed kick but nevertheless is a tremendous asset. Practice power kicks using both techniques, using both the instep and the ball of the foot as weapons.

SLIDING BACK SWING KICK

The Swing Kick–Roundhouse Kick double technique has won many a point in competition. The key is proper execution of the Swing Kick, which is a slashing type of kick like the Roundhouse Kick. The slow-motion drill should be done as follows.

1. From a side stance, slide the rear foot up to the front foot, turning the rear foot so that the toes are pointing to the rear, as in the Side Kick.
2. Also, as in the Side Kick, raise, or channel, the knee so that the heel is pointing directly at the target.
3. Slowly move the weapon toward the target, but instead of aiming at the head with the heel, aim about one head's width to the side of the head (on a right-leg kick, aim about one head's width to the left of your opponent's head), and when the leg is fully extended, allow the foot to continue moving until it is in a position similar to that of the front kick.
4. Sweep, or slash, the weapon (ball of the foot) through the target and hold for five seconds.
5. Return to the channeled position.
6. Return to the side stance.

If you've never done this drill before, you shouldn't be disappointed if you can't put your weapon on the head of your opponent. The object is to build up strength so that you can do this in the future. Do five repetitions on each leg. Follow with 15 full-speed kicks on each leg. It is helpful if you have a partner holding something as a focus target, so that you can get the feel of the foot going through the target.

SLIDING BACK SWING KICK, side view: Start in the side stance **(A)** and slide up (note position of rear foot) **(B)**. Channel the weapon **(C)** and move it to the side of the target's head **(D)**. Swing through, keeping your leg straight **(E)**.

HOOK KICK

The Hook Kick is a variation of the Swing Kick that is used at closer range. Slow-motion drills follow those of the Swing Kick up to step 4. Instead of slashing through the target, keeping the leg straight, and rolling the hip as in the Swing Kick, you bend the knee and hit the opponent with the ball or heel of the foot. Now continue the drill:

5. Return to the channeled position.
6. Return to the side stance.

As in the other kicks, do this drill five times on each leg and follow with 15 full-speed kicks. You might find this one difficult at first, especially when you kick at the air, but don't give up.

HOOK KICK, last part: First follow steps A, B, C, and D. Then **(E)**, send the weapon out beside the target's head, then hook to the head **(F)**.

BACK KICK

A Back Kick–Roundhouse Kick combination is a good weapon because the Back Kick is generally considered a power kick, and many opponents don't expect a slashing follow-up kick. Execution, again, is the main objective of slow-motion drills.

1. From the side stance, left side forward, turn your body to the right, at the same time turning your head and pivoting your feet, until your back is to the target and you are looking over your right shoulder at the target.
2. Channel the leg in a position similar to that of the Side Kick but with the knee drawn in tighter as though you were trying to touch it to your left shoulder.
3. Slowly extend the weapon (the heel) to the target and hold for five seconds (at full-extension the kick looks just like a Side Kick).
4. Return to the channeled position.
5. Return to the side stance.

BACK KICK, side view: Starting in the side stance **(A)**, turn to the left **(B)**, pivot the feet, and turn your head to look over your right shoulder. Channel the weapon (the knee is in tighter than for the side kick) **(C)**, execute the kick to the target **(D)**, and return.

B

C

D

Practice the slow-motion drill five times on each side, looking at yourself in a mirror, if possible, so that you can train yourself to look at the target *before* you kick. Many people make the mistake of kicking and then looking. When you are working on the one-count full-speed focus kicks, be sure to concentrate on recoil. Bring the weapon back along the same track it took on the way out.

Generally you should go through the basics during every workout. One good way is to follow stretching drills with a series of basic kicks, which not only will serve to reinforce good basics but also will further warm up your body in preparation for multiple-kick drills. Never take a casual attitude while going through the basics. Instead, try to make each kick the perfect one. Your overall karate skills will benefit greatly.

4

Double Kicks

Basically, double-kick combinations are designed for two purposes: to beat a counteroffensive fighter, who comes off a single kick attack with a counter technique; and as an offensive-minded strategy that forces an opponent to block in one direction while a follow-up technique hits his open area.

Becoming proficient at double-kick techniques will help the slower or smaller fighter offset speed and height disadvantages, and it will make the gifted athlete excel, possibly beyond his imagination.

Once you've practiced a few double-kick combinations you'll understand the unwavering attention paid to the basics in the previous chapters.

There will be 10 combinations in this chapter, but in actuality you are limited only by the scope of your imagination. These combinations are proven in tournament competition.

ROUND KICK-SIDE KICK

The Round Kick is one of the most frequently used kicks in a

ROUND KICK–SIDE KICK: Start in the side stance **(A)** and slide up **(B)**. Execute a Round Kick to the head **(C)**, which draws the high block **(D)**; rechamber quickly for the Side Kick **(E** and **F)**; and execute **(G)**.

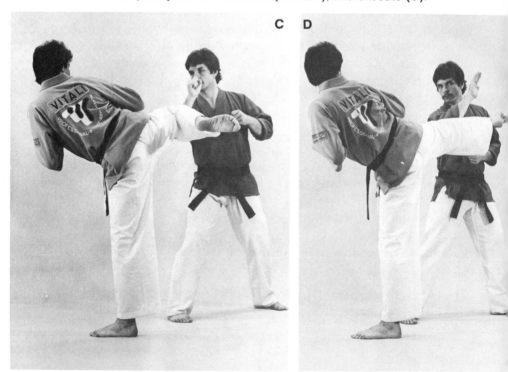

E

fighter's arsenal. Because of that, most fighters develop effective defenses against it. The Round Kick's circular delivery makes it easier to block than other kicks because it doesn't come at you in a straight line. By throwing a Side Kick after a Round Kick, a fighter can effectively learn to keep counterpunchers at a disadvantage. The key is to chamber quickly from the Round-Kick position to the Side-Kick position by shifting the leg and body so that the heel is on a straight line with the target. Also, don't use perfect Round-Kick technique. Instead of a full pivot of the supporting foot, only pivot half as much as usual, which will be of great aid in maintaining your balance. To develop this technique properly, work with a partner and have him block the primary (Round Kick), then counter with a Reverse Punch, Back Fist, etc., while you deliver a controlled Side Kick. Practice chambering into the Side-Kick position from the Round Kick in front of a mirror in slow motion.

F   G

SIDE KICK–ROUND KICK

This technique works best against two types of fighters, the one who evades the kick (backs up, leans back) and counters and the fighter who tries to jam a Side Kick with his arm with a follow-up technique in mind. Kicking focus pads with the Side Kick–Round Kick combination will help you develop the balance needed as well as the snap and speed of the Round Kick. The idea is to kick into the air with the Side Kick and hit the focus pad, which your partner is holding at head level. Work particularly hard on chambering from the Side Kick to the Round Kick and remember to use that little hip action to put power into the Round Kick.

SIDE KICK–ROUND KICK: Start in the side stance **(A)** and slide up **(B)**. Execute a Side Kick **(C)**, drawing your guard low **(D)**; quickly rechamber for a Round Kick **(E)**, and hit high **(F)**.

C

D

BACK-LEG ROUND KICK–SIDE KICK

To work properly, this technique has to be set up. You do so by executing a Back-Leg Round Kick that forces some kind of block. Now that you have made your opponent anticipate the Round Kick, he will automatically block, which will open up a target (rib cage) for the Side Kick. Again, most counterfighters favor coming off the Round Kick more than any other because the circular motion of that kick leaves him a safer, more open path to your body as your kick recoils. This is the illusion you want to present so that he runs into your Side Kick.

A   B

BACK-LEG ROUND KICK–SIDE KICK: Execute a Back-Leg Round Kick **(A, B,** and **C)**, drawing the guard high **(D)**, then rechamber quickly **(E)** and hit low with a Side Kick **(F)**.

E   F

DOUBLE SIDE KICK

The Side Kick, when properly delivered, is hard to defend against. Therefore, many fighters' strategy against this kick is quite simply to evade it instead of blocking it. Take a few Side Kicks on the arm, and you'll understand the pain of blocking it often. The idea is to back up or lean back just enough and then follow the kick's recoil with a counter technique. The second Side Kick is designed especially for this kind of fighter. Working with kicking shields will help you develop the timing and power needed in the second kick. Execute the first kick, recoil, and, as your partner moves in (as though he were countering), kick into the shield. Move too quickly and the kick is ineffective, too slowly and it will be jammed. Timing is critical on this kick.

SIDE KICK–SIDE KICK: Execute a Side Kick **(A, B,** and **C)**, which your opponent will evade **(D)**, and as he rushes with a counteroffensive move **(E)**, hit with the second Side Kick **(F)**.

SIDE KICK LOW–SIDE KICK HIGH

This is a variation of the Double Side Kick. You set up this kick with a Double Side Kick, and when your opponent comes in with a counter he will have his guard low to block the second kick. Instead of going to the midsection, though, you catch him with his guard down and kick him in the face. If successful, this kick should end any confrontation.

SIDE KICK LOW–SIDE KICK HIGH: When your opponent is expecting a Double Side Kick **(A, B, C,** and **D)** he will counterattack with his guard low to protect his midsection **(E)**. This is the time to Side Kick High on the second part of the combination **(F)**.

SWING KICK–ROUND KICK

Because the Swing Kick resembles the Side Kick in the early stages of execution, your opponent is already somewhat off guard because he has to figure out what technique you are using. Therefore, he is more off balance than usual when the Swing Kick is delivered. Generally, he will step back or lean back as the kick swings through and then come back with a counter. This is when the Round Kick hits him. Remembering to keep the leg straight as it swings through the Swing Kick, merely bend the knee 45 degrees as it passes the head and immediately come back with the Round Kick. Use hip action to offset the lack of leg movement.

SWING KICK–ROUND KICK: **(A, B, C, D,** and **E)** Your opponent will evade the first technique (Swing Kick). As he is moving toward you for the counterattack, hit with the Swing Kick **(F)**.

C

D

E

F

FRONT KICK–ROUND KICK

As in the Back-Leg Round Kick–Side Kick, you need to set up your opponent to make this combination work. In this case the idea is to catch him with a Front Kick to the midsection, causing him to drop his protection, then rechamber quickly and deliver the Round Kick. The key here is to rechamber and then pivot your supporting foot to increase the hip motion as you deliver the kick.

A   B

FRONT KICK–ROUND KICK: The Front Kick **(A, B,** and **C)** will make the opponent drop his guard, leaving the head open for the follow-up Round Kick **(D, E,** and **F).**

C

D

FAKE ROUND KICK–HOOK KICK

The key to this combination is to make the fake believable; otherwise it is doomed. You have to execute the fake with a commitment or it will be ignored. Once the opponent buys the fake, swing your leg through without actually completing the Round Kick and Hook Kick to the other side of the opponent's head.

A   **B**

FAKE ROUND KICK–HOOK KICK: Send a Round Kick at the midsection **(A, B, C,** and **D)** and, at the last second, rechamber **(E)** and Hook Kick to the opposite side of your opponent's head **(F** and **G)**.

C

D

G

FAKE SWING KICK-ROUND KICK

The fake must be believable so that the opponent will move back in preparation for a counter instead of moving in quickly with a defensive technique. Move in as though you were going to hit with a single Swing Kick, and as the opponent reacts, quickly rechamber for the Round Kick and execute. This is nearly the same as the Swing Kick-Round Kick combination except that the kicking leg doesn't straighten, and the Round Kick hits more quickly.

A

B

FAKE SWING KICK–ROUND KICK: After you have set up a Swing Kick **(A, B, C,** and **D)**, your opponent should take the fake **(E)**, which will set him up for the quick Round Kick that follows **(F)**.

C

D

COUNTERING SLIDING ROUND KICK WITH SPINNING BACK KICK

Correct timing is the key to this move. As your opponent slides into the chambered position, you must immediately begin your technique and have it delivered before his is on the way. Not only will you have an effective counter; your opponent will think twice about using a Round Kick; thus you take away a weapon from *his* arsenal.

These are but a few of many combinations that can increase your skill and the number of trophies in your cabinet. Once you get the idea it is not inconceivable to make up combinations as you go along when the opportunities present themselves.

Keep working on them and you'll soon be through that discouraging period of awkwardness and really start stinging them.

SPINNING BACK KICK COUNTER TO ROUND KICK: As the opponent begins to slide up and chamber for a Round Kick **(A, B,** and **C)**, quickly spin **(D)** and deliver a Back Kick **(E)**. Timing is the key factor.

A

5

Kicks with Punches

There are very few fighters in the world today who can connect with a single kicking technique, no matter how fast the kick, no matter how good the kicker. There is too much distance from the floor to the target, and the leg moves slower than the arm or fist. Even under belts can avoid most single kicks. Only in the movies or on television, where fight scenes are carefully choreographed, will you see a fighter execute a single kick and score.

If you can't hit someone with a kick, why work so hard on them? It's a good question. Kicks are still by far more powerful than punches, and they have more range, which is a decided advantage to a smaller person fighting a big opponent, but he has to set up his kicks or die trying.

One of the best ways to hit with a kick is to combine it with punches—and vice versa. You use deception as a magician would, causing your opponent to look in one direction while you are attacking from another.

Don't be misled by the idea that faking is a simple proposition. Fakes must appear to be real. They must be believable, and the best way to ensure that believability is to develop good hand techniques. Your opponent must respect the hand technique or he will ignore it. You should develop a good jab, Back Fist, or Reverse Punch or all three and deliver the fakes of those punches as though they were the actual punches themselves. Imagine to yourself that the punch is real. If *you* believe it, your opponent definitely will. The object of the fake is to cause the opponent to react in one direction, while you slip in another technique from another. There is, however, always the chance that the first technique will work, so you must go for the first strike and then follow up. As you progress with these techniques, of course, you will begin to "read" your opponents and instinctively know when a fake is going to work and when you should try another technique.

Here are a few techniques to give you a start. They aren't iron-clad, but they work. There are as many combinations as your mind can contain; it's merely a matter of inventing them and perfecting them.

BACK FIST–SIDE KICK

This is a technique that can be used over and over with success. The idea is to execute the Back Fist, causing the opponent to raise his guard, exposing an opening in the rib cage. As you deliver the Back Fist, slide your rear foot up to your front foot and execute the kick as you are recoiling the Back Fist. Sometimes the opening will be as small as the width of a foot, so it is important to be accurate and quick. Also, there are times when the Back Fist will be so good that the opponent can't stop it. In those cases, hit him!

BACK FIST–SIDE KICK: Lead with the Back Fist (**A** and **B**), sliding the rear foot up (**C**) and channeling for the Side Kick (**D**). Execute and recoil (**E** and **F**), maintaining readiness for the counter.

C

D

E

F

CRESCENT KICK–HIGH PUNCH

This time you lead with a kick and make an opening for a punch, and there might be more than one way that the kick will open up your opponent. Execute a sliding Crescent Kick to the head, forcing your opponent to guard the side of his head (usually, he will use both arms). The punch is delivered to his head as soon as your foot touches the floor. It is obvious that you must work hard on maintaining as much of an upright stance as possible, and you must react quickly when your foot touches down. There is a chance that the kick will hit your opponent's arms as it sweeps through, dragging them down and clearing his face momentarily. This is a golden opportunity and must be followed quickly. There isn't a great chance of scoring with the

CRESCENT KICK–HIGH PUNCH: Lead with the sliding Crescent Kick (**A** and **B**), maintaining an upright body position (**C, D,** and **E**), and follow with a punch to the head (**F**).

A

B

C

D

E

F

Crescent, but that disadvantage is compensated for by the reaction—"Kick!"—in your opponent's head that slows his reactions.

BACK FIST–MIDDLE ROUND KICK–HIGH PUNCH

The idea is to create an opening for a high punch after you have been delivering two-move combinations for some time. You lead with the Back Fist to make your opponent react, follow with the Middle Round Kick to draw his guard downward, leaving his face open for the High Punch. The high-low-high combination is a surprise, too, since you have been delivering one-two moves before. To score with the High Punch, you must begin the punch even before your foot touches down so that it will land as the foot touches or slightly before. You can see that it is important to keep the body upright while kicking, or the punch will have to travel too far to be effective.

A

BACK FIST–ROUND KICK–HIGH PUNCH: Lead with the Back Fist **(A** and **B)**, sliding the rear leg forward to set up the Round Kick **(C)**; execute the kick **(D** and **E)** and follow with the High Punch **(F)**.

B

BACK FIST-MIDDLE ROUND KICK-SPINNING BACK KICK

He's seen the first two moves before, and if he's quick, he might come at you with a counter off the Round Kick, or he might lean back to avoid the punch he thinks will follow and then counter. You have him either way. Be sure to have your Round Kick weapon going into position to become the supporting foot for the Back Kick. As soon as the Round Kick strikes, recoil and drop it directly to the floor while the kicking foot for the Back Kick is being chambered. You will either hit your opponent as he leans away from the imagined punch, or he will rush into the kick. It scores either way.

BACK FIST-MIDDLE ROUND KICK-SPINNING BACK KICK: Lead with the Back Fist **(A)**, sliding the rear foot up to set up the Round Kick **(B)**. Execute the Round Kick **(C and D)**, recoil **(E)**, place the foot down **(F)** to facilitate the Round Kick position, and execute **(G, H, and I)**.

A

B

C

F

G

BACK FIST-SWING KICK-HIGH PUNCH

Keeping your opponent off balance, confused, is the name of the game, whether you're in the ring, in the street, or even in business. While he's guessing what you are about to do, he's not thinking about what *he's* going to do. The object this time, of course, is to clear the area for a High Punch. Leading with the Back Fist again (he must react or you simply hit him), compound the pressure with a sliding Swing Kick to the head, which also might strike him, knock down his guard, or cause him to lean back. Start the High Punch even before the kicking foot has touched down, trying to land the punch slightly before the foot touches or just as it touches. The timing is important for a good punch. Again, it is important to keep your body as upright as possible for quick follow-up with the punch.

As you might have noticed, there have been several combinations so far, and the high-low or punch-kick sequences have all

BACK FIST-SWING KICK-HIGH PUNCH: Lead with the Back Fist **(A** and **B)**, sliding the rear foot up to set up the Swing Kick **(C)**. Execute the Swing Kick (change of perspective to see last kick) **(D, E, F,** and **G)**, maintaining an upright body position, then touch down and punch **(H, I,** and **J)**.

A

B

C

D

E

F G

H I

J

varied. Your opponent should really be thinking by now, wondering what will come at him next—a foot or a fist, high or low? If this is the case, you are in control, and that's another objective gained.

BACK FIST–BACK FIST–SLIDING ROUND KICK–MIDDLE PUNCH

Logically, four-move combinations follow three-move ones, but it isn't a must. It all depends on how your earlier combinations have worked. By delivering two Back Fists, you are again breaking up sequence, continuing to confuse your opponent. He was probably looking for a kick to follow that first Back Fist, and now he's backing away from a Sliding Round Kick, covering as well as he can. The Middle Punch should score easily. The Middle Punch must hit as your foot touches or slightly before.

One step beyond multiple punch-kick combinations are the "touch" techniques. These are simply a matter of kicking, touching down, and quickly delivering another kick—just another way to catch an opponent by surprise. Your opponent is in the process of a counter to a two-move combination when the surprise third move hits. The key to this technique is to work on quickly touching down and kicking. Don't drop your foot and stomp, drop it quickly, and barely touch before it is on its way again. This will take a lot of practice.

BACK FIST-BACK FIST-SLIDING ROUND KICK-MIDDLE PUNCH:
Execute the Back Fist **(A)**, recoil **(B)**, and Back Fist again **(C)**, sliding the
rear foot up **(D)** with a punch to set up the Round Kick. Execute the kick,
maintaining an upright body position **(E** and **F)**, and follow with the
Middle Punch **(G** and **H)**.

E

F

G

H

BACK FIST-SIDE KICK-TOUCH-SIDE KICK

Suppose your opponent has seen the Back Fist–Side Kick combination several times and is beginning to have some success at either blocking it or avoiding it. This time, deliver the combination—maybe even slow down the Side Kick slightly to draw him in—and then, as your opponent either relaxes, leans back, or rushes to counter, touch down and Side Kick again. Don't worry if the kick doesn't extend the full distance when an opponent charges you, because his momentum adds power to your kick.

SIDE KICK-TOUCH-SIDE KICK: Lead with the Back Fist **(A** and **B)**, sliding the rear foot up to set up the Side Kick and close distance **(C)**. Execute **(D** and **E)**, recoil **(F)**, and touch down **(G)**, immediately executing the second Side Kick **(H)**.

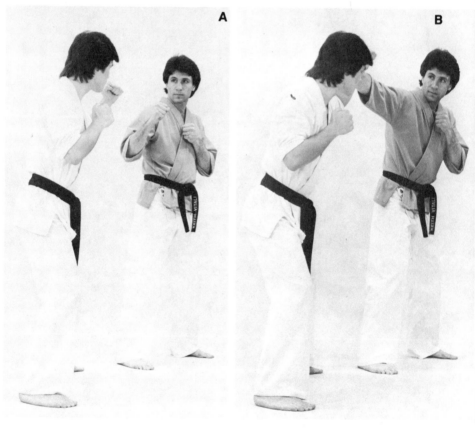

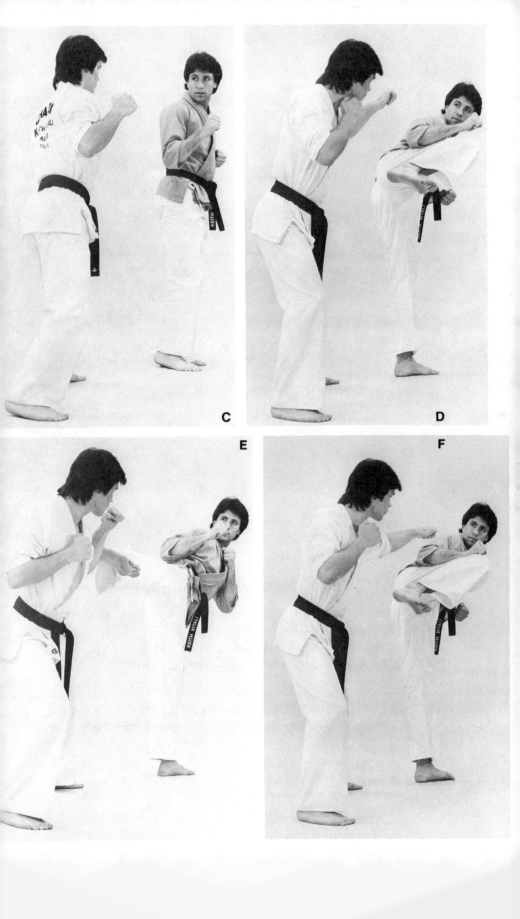

C

D

E

F

G   H

BACK FIST–SIDE KICK–TOUCH–HOOK KICK

Here again the high-low, low-high theory is at work. Your opponent might be looking for a second Side Kick this time, so make the follow-up kick a Hook Kick to the head. This works best against someone who is going to counter after the first kick.

SIDE KICK–TOUCH–HOOK KICK: Lead with the Back Fist **(A and B)**, sliding the rear foot up to set up the Side Kick **(C)**; execute the Side Kick **(D and E)**, touch down **(F and G)**, and immediately execute the Hook Kick **(H, I and J)**.

A

B

C

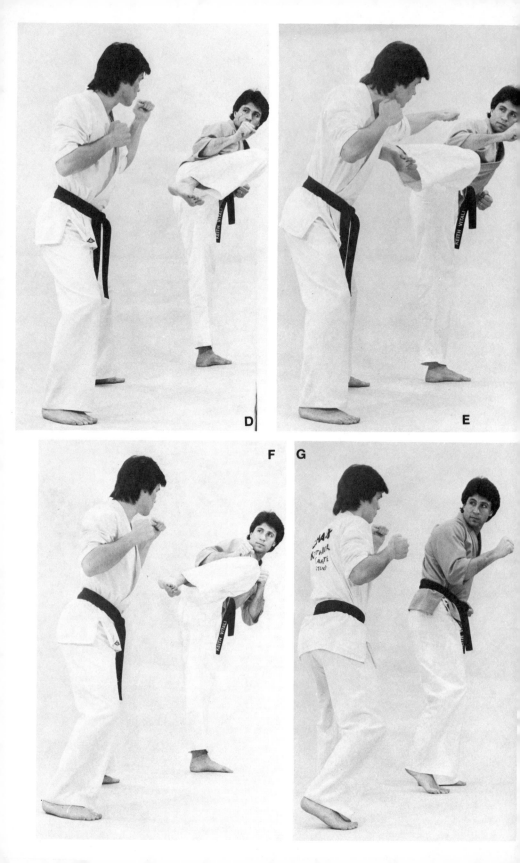

H   I

J

REVERSE PUNCH–ROUND KICK–TOUCH–SIDE KICK

Because of the distance between weapon and target on both the Reverse Punch and the Round Kick, your opponent might be able to avoid each technique. He also might relax after the Round Kick and set himself up perfectly for the Touch–Side Kick that follows. This will work especially well against someone who is countering.

All of these combinations are proven in tournament competition against top-10 opponents, but they aren't the only ones by any means. The idea is to have a number of combinations in your head—or, you might say, put several scenarios into your computer—so that when you are in the ring or confronted with a situation on the street you aren't left wondering what to do while you are being dismantled.

You must practice any combination until it flows from one technique to the next and each technique is a weapon unto itself. You never know which technique might score, so you want to deliver each one with speed, focus, and power.

If you learn the nine combinations in this chapter and execute them well, you will score points in the ring or hit someone in a self-defense situation. Practice them until you have complete confidence in each move of each combination, because your opponent can read your lack of confidence with no trouble at all, and if he does, the time was spent for nothing.

HIGH PUNCH–ROUND KICK–TOUCH–SIDE KICK: Lead with the Reverse Punch (**A** and **B**), flowing into a Round Kick (**C** and **D**); touch down (**E** and **F**) and immediately execute a Side Kick (**G** and **H**).

D

E

6

Additional Training Information

Now that you have some idea of what to do, the next step should be to perfect your technique. There are many ways to become good at something, but they all boil down to one thing in the end—repetition. So, the best way to learn something is to find the drill that makes repetition easier to take.

PARTNER KICKING

One of the best ways to build up your kicking muscles, other than doing actual kicking drills, is through partner kicks, a drill taught to me by Bill Wallace, the retired, undefeated Professional Karate Association world middleweight champion and the man they called "Superfoot." These drills are quick and productive.

Both partners face each other, same side forward. Partner A holds Partner B's hand, and Partner B raises his knee as high as possible into the Round Kick position (keeping his knee in line with his partner). Partner B executes 25 Round Kicks without putting down his leg, emphasizing recoil on each kick. He should bend his body no more than 45 degrees from the hips because his partner is holding him up and balance is no problem. After Partner B finishes his kicks Partner A takes his turn, and then the two switch sides and repeat the drill. Now repeat the kicks without holding your partner's hand. Where speed and height were the objects before, balance is what you're working on now.

We use this drill often, inserting it in between other types of drills during a night's workout. Eventually you will want to work up to 50 kicks holding hands and on your own.

PARTNER KICKS: Holding your partner's hand, execute a Round Kick to the head **(A** and **B)** (or as high as possible), then to the midsection **(C** and **D)**, then to the groin area **(E** and **F)**; or execute all kicks to a high level **(G)**.

C

D

G

SLOW-MOTION DRILLS

As with the partner kicks, Partner A and Partner B hold hands, facing each other with the same side forward. Once you lift your leg on this drill you must not put it down until the entire drill is completed. Partner A slowly executes a Round Kick to Partner B's head, then rechambers into the Side Kick and delivers a controlled Side Kick, then chambers into the Hook Kick position and delivers a slow-motion Hook Kick to the head. Repeat this five times before putting your foot down. Partner B takes his turn, and then both partners repeat the drill with the opposite legs. After both sides are worked out, repeat without holding hands for five more repetitions on each side.

After doing these drills for about a month you'll definitely notice an improvement in your kicking ability.

A

SLOW-MOTION DRILL: Slowly execute a Round Kick to the head **(A** and **B),** recoil slowly **(C)**, rechannel for the Side Kick **(D)**, kick and recoil slowly **(E** and **F)**, rechannel for the Hook Kick **(G)**, execute the kick **(H** and **I)**, and recoil slowly **(J)**.

B

E

F

G

H

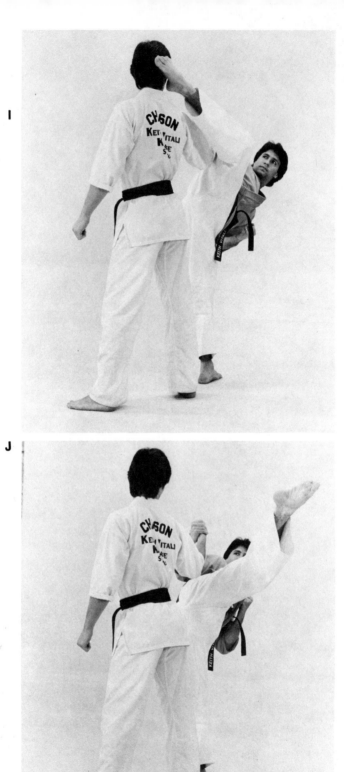

THE 1,000-KICK DRILL

This might sound impossible. Tough, yes; impossible, no. The 1,000-kick drill is designed for people who hate to keep count. By the time you have finished this drill you will have done 1,000 kicks. The idea is that if you practice anything 1,000 times a day, whatever it is, you will become good at it in spite of yourself.

There are thousands of combinations and kicks you could work with, so the best idea is to take four to eight kicks and just hit them 1,000 times. Do them with a partner so they don't become monotonous. Do them back and forth, developing a rhythm, a sense of timing and distance, because you have a partner to aim at.

Start with stretches, then follow with single kicks. Pick four single kicks to work with, such as a Front Kick, a Sliding Round Kick, a Side Kick, and a Swing Kick. Do 15 repetitions.

Follow this with partner kicks, 50 repetitions on each leg. Be sure to bend the knee at least 45 degrees and kick as high as possible. After kicking with both legs, repeat the sequence without holding hands for balance. What you are doing here is building up the kicking muscles in the legs, plus gaining balance.

Following the static drills, go into double-kick drills. Again, pick four combinations you want to use—Side Kick–Round Kick, Round Kick–Side Kick, Round Kick–Round Kick, Swing Kick–Round Kick, etc.—and do 15 repetitions with each leg.

Follow that with a repeat of partner kicks. Next, work on triple kicks such as triple Round Kicks (to any part of the body), Side Kick–Round Kick–Side Kick, Swing Kick–Round Kick–Side Kick, etc. When you have finished the last of your triple kicks, count them. You'll discover that you have done more than 1,000 kicks. Do them every day for a while, and you'll be amazed at the improvement as your kicks become higher and higher, faster and faster.

CIRCLE KICKS

This is done with a circle of more than three people. The idea is that you can throw a technique at a partner, who does not counter but merely tries to defend the kick. You can work on the execution of the kick without being fearful of a counterattack. It also gives the second man a chance to practice blocking. Rotate kicks in a circle over and over. Do any kind of kick you want. The whole idea is to learn kicking techniques in a controlled situation. You might want to develop a Spinning Swing Kick, for instance, but you know you'll get clubbed if you try it on the mat. In this type of drill, however, you get to practice that kick over and over until you're good enough to use it. When you're good enough to hit anybody in the circle, then's when you take it out on the mat.

All of these techniques have been proven. Not only do they improve your kicking techniques; they have also helped fighters garner trophies from tournaments nationwide, and they have been seen to be effective on nationally televised demonstrations and in a self-defense situation or two.

Stick with it and success will be yours.

Index